SPORTS BIOGRAPHIES

CONOR MCGREGOR

KENNY ABDO

Fly!
An Imprint of Abdo Zoom
abdobooks.com

abdobooks.com

Published by Abdo Zoom, a division of ABDO, P.O. Box 398166, Minneapolis,
Minnesota 55439. Copyright © 2019 by Abdo Consulting Group, Inc. International
copyrights reserved in all countries. No part of this book may be reproduced in any
form without written permission from the publisher. Fly!™ is a trademark and logo
of Abdo Zoom.

Printed in the United States of America, North Mankato, Minnesota.
052018
092018

**THIS BOOK CONTAINS
RECYCLED MATERIALS**

Photo Credits: Alamy, AP Images, Icon Sportswire, iStock
Production Contributors: Kenny Abdo, Jennie Forsberg, Grace Hansen
Design Contributors: Dorothy Toth, Neil Klinepier

Library of Congress Control Number: 2017960655

Publisher's Cataloging-in-Publication Data

Names: Abdo, Kenny, author.
Title: Conor McGregor / by Kenny Abdo.
Description: Minneapolis, Minnesota : Abdo Zoom, 2019. | Series: Sports biographies |
    Includes online resources and index.
Identifiers: ISBN 9781532124778 (lib.bdg.) | ISBN 9781532124914 (ebook) |
    ISBN 9781532124983 (Read-to-me ebook)
Subjects: LCSH: McGregor, Conor--1988-, Biography--Juvenile literature. |
    Martial artists--Ireland--Biography--Juvenile literature. |
    Ultimate Fighting Championship (Organization)--Biography-- Juvenile literature.
Classification: DDC 796.815 [B]--dc23

TABLE OF CONTENTS

CONOR MCGREGOR

Conor McGregor went from fighting schoolyard bullies to fighting in mixed martial arts (MMA) professionally.

He is the only fighter to be a **champion** in two Ultimate Fighting Championship (UFC) **divisions** at the same time.

EARLY YEARS

McGregor was born in Dublin, Ireland in 1988.

He has always enjoyed sports, especially soccer and boxing. At age 12, McGregor began boxing at a local **club**.

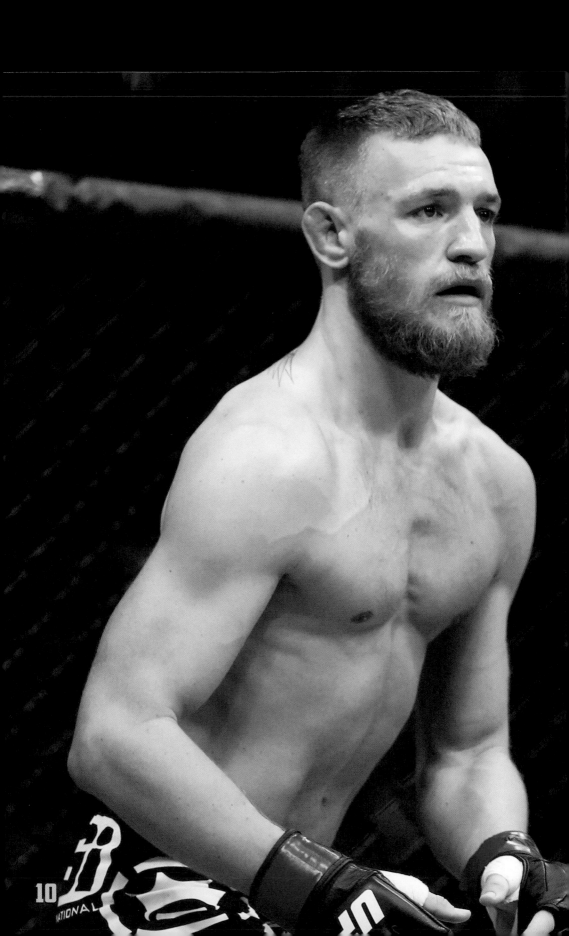

While working as a plumber, he met future UFC fighter Tom Egan. They started to train in MMA together.

GOING PRO

McGregor's first professional MMA **bout** was in 2008.

After a few fights, he considered another career. But his mother encouraged him to stick with the sport.

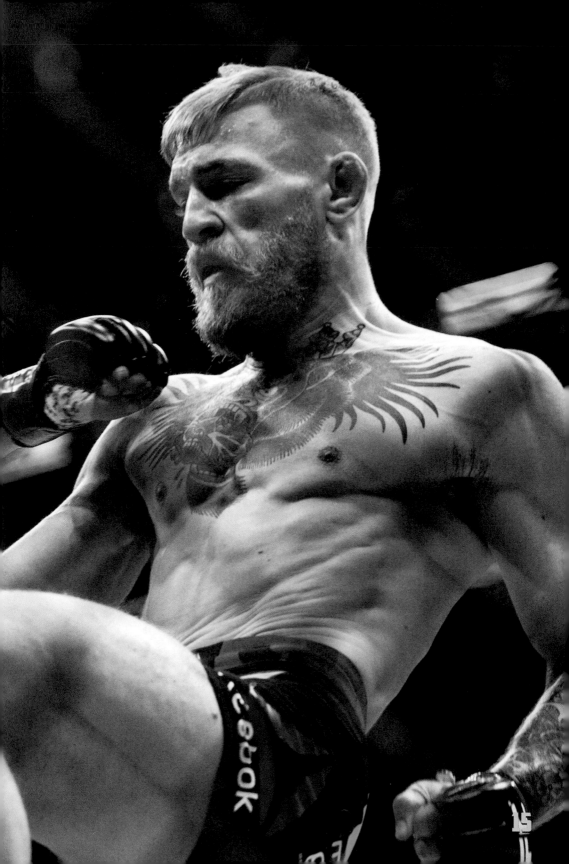

McGregor signed with UFC as a fighter in 2013. His fastest recorded **knockout** in the UFC was an amazing 13 seconds.

During a fight with Max Holloway, McGregor tore his **ACL** but still won the match. The injury kept him from fighting until 2014. He returned to the ring and dominated.

In 2017, McGregor took a break from MMA to focus on boxing. He fought and lost to Floyd Mayweather Jr. in one of the most-watched Pay-Per-View matches of all time. McGregor returned to MMA, but said he was willing to box again.

LEGACY

McGregor has been featured on television, in film, and many video games. He also has his own clothing line, called August McGregor.

McGregor is a strong supporter of the **equal rights movement**.

GLOSSARY

ACL – short for anterior cruciate ligament, one of the main muscles that stabilizes the knee joint.

bout – a wrestling or boxing match.

champion – the winner of a championship, which is a match held to find a first-place winner.

club – a place dedicated to a certain activity.

division – a group of people who compete against each other for a championship.

equal rights movement – an effort to guarantee equal rights for every citizen.

knockout – legal fight-ending strike that keeps an opponent from continuing the match.

ONLINE RESOURCES

 Booklinks
NONFICTION NETWORK
FREE! ONLINE NONFICTION RESOURCES

To learn more about Conor McGregor, please visit **abdobooklinks.com**. These links are routinely monitored and updated to provide the most current information available.

INDEX